ENTREPENEAURSHIP
IT'S A STRUGGLE
BUT YOU CAN MAKE IT

BY LEONARD HAYES

Copyright 2007 by Leonard Hayes.

ISBN 978-1-59916-342-0

DEDICATION

First of all I give glory to God for given me this God given talent for Business. I dedicate this book to my Mom. Thank you for your love and Support and for being the best mom In the world to me... To my wife Gia Thank you for your love and support. And to my 5 daily inspirations: André, Octavia, Paige AAerion and Kyle. Continue to make your dad proud. Work hard seek God and you can overcome any obstacles this world throws at you.

ACKNOWLEDGEMENT

First of all I want to acknowledge Two of the most influential men in my Life. Pastor Carl Randle of Fair Haven COGIC; Pastor thanks for your Wisdom, your spiritual teachings and just being my friend. You've been there for me through the rough times and you've really shown me the true meaning of a great Shepard and true friend. Pastor I'm forever grateful.

And to My current Pastor Dr. Carl King Sr. of Christ Community COGIC. Pastor thank you for welcoming me into the fold. Thank you for being not only a great Pastor but a great friend, golfing buddy, and excellent teacher of the gospel.

And to all my true friends and colleagues thanks for your support.

PROLOGUE

Leonard Hayes was born in the city of Chicago, Despite being raised in the Robert Taylor Homes one of the roughest Chicago housing projects despite being surrounded by gangs, drugs crime and poverty he work hard and beat the odds. By the age of 30 he owned and operated a clothing store, 2 cellular stores 2 mattress retail store. A mattress manufacturing company. A fast food restaurant a carpet store, a construction company and currently owns one of the largest mortgage companies in the southern suburbs he's also the President of AM Title services and New Vision construction. If you're a future entrepreneur struggling entrepreneur or if you're inspired to be an entrepreneur this quick read is for you.

6

TABLE OF CONTENTS

Chapter 1
When I knew I had the gift..................9

Chapter 2
Entrepreneurs are smart followers and excellent Leaders......................15

Chapter 3
Another Mans Junk is a Entrepreneurs treasure....................27

Chapter 4
Count up the cost before you take a lost. 35

Chapter 5
Business and family don't mix..........47

Chapter 6
Leave the leeches behind...................57

Chapter 7
Know when to fold em.......................67

Chapter 8
When your back is against the wall ..77

Chapter 9
Taking no prisoners 87

Chapter 10
A new vision 105

Chapter 1:

When I Knew I Had the Gift

Growing up with nine brothers and sisters was tough, but growing up in the Chicago Housing Projects was tougher. Imagine a family of nine living off of $450 in cash and $500 in food stamps, which had to last for a whole month. Just imagine getting two pairs of shoes a year; a pair of gym shoes and a pair of school shoes, which had to last you all year. And when the soles wore out you had to stuff your shoe with cardboard and plastic just to protect your feet from the elements.

But I wouldn't change a thing about me growing up, because that taught me about survival. My mother use to give me a dollar a month for allowance, but back then; you could really make a dollar stretch. I remember one hot summer day I got tired of being broke and decided to do something about it.

Remember: one basic thing about being an entrepreneur is that it's about getting a product that's in demand and finding the clientele to sell it to.

I was ten years old and I came up with an idea to capitalize on the 100-degree summer day. I took my $1 and started my first business.

I went to the store and bought two packs of Kool-Aid for twenty cents and a pack of 50 Styrofoam cups for fifty-nine cents. I went home and borrowed some sugar from my neighbor (yeah borrowed that's what we did in the projects, we was broke) and I made twenty ice cups and sold them for ten cents each. I made a whole two dollars in a matter of three hours, and guess what my ice cups were in demand. I know what you are thinking, wow a whole two dollars but I want you to look at the big picture. It was an idea that made an instant profit. And it was a business venture. From that day I knew I was different, my mind was always on how to make a dollar grow.

I remember one Christmas when I was twelve the hand held video game came out. Needless to say my mom couldn't afford to buy one for me and my little brother, but I came up with another brilliant business venture. I put together five dollars and went to five of my friends and rented there hand held video game for a day for .50 cents each, which cost me $2.50. I bought a bag of popcorn kernels for .69 cents. I went home and made a sign which read; game room open .25 cents a game, a free bag of butter popcorn and cup of Kool-Aid with each game. I decorated my mom's living room with balloons and the game room was open. I had at least 15 to 20 kids come through my make shift game room, and I made $25.00 that day. Needless to say all of the kids that I rented the games from came and paid to play their own games as well. Now did I take advantage of my peers? No. Was it a great business venture? Yes. I made 200% profit in one day.

The point I am trying to make is to be an entrepreneur you always have to be a thinker and you have to seize the moment and play the game with the cards you're dealt with.

I came up with a product that was in demand and I targeted a certain clientele. Even at an early age I realized that my clientele was my peers. I just had to find out what they liked and bring the product to them, with a little twist. Keep in mind we all were friends and they had the video games, but I have the game room concept, and the popcorn and Kool-Aid as the twist. The same method works today. Our peers are our clientele, we just have to find a product that they want and bring it to them with a twist.

Chapter 2:

Entrepreneurs are Smart Followers and Excellent Leaders

Now that you know how I got started, let's define what an entrepreneur really is. Webster's dictionary defines an entrepreneur as "<u>one who initiates or finance new commercial enterprise or economic ventures</u>". Sound kind of vague don't you think? My definition is "anyone who takes a product, finds a demand for that product, and finds clients to purchase that product for the purpose of making a profit for themselves". That's a simple enough definition don't you think?

We all know or ran across many entrepreneurs in our life time. For example: that person driving though the alley with his pick-up truck, collecting scrap metal to take to the junk yard. Or that person that stands out in the middle of the intersection selling ice cold bottled water on a hot summer day. Better yet, who can forget the guy on public transportation selling tube socks, three packs for a dollar? I remember I use to see those individuals and I use to say, man why don't they get a real job, and you probably said the same thing. But as I grew older I realized they were more courageous than any one who had a 9 to 5. They went out and created there own jobs, and that takes courage. Whether you want to admit it or not, they are true entrepreneurs. While growing up, I quickly realized that I didn't know all the answers, but if you show me enough times, I will eventually figure it out. This brought me to another business venture.

As a child, one of my favorite pass times was eating candy – which was the pass time for 90% of the kids in my housing project. I remember frequently visiting our local candy lady, Mrs. Hudson – she sold candy out of her house.

We had to look through her screen door to tell her what kind of candy we wanted. I know this may seem kind of odd, but someone robbed her at gunpoint, consequently, she didn't trust anyone to enter into her home. But Mrs. Hudson was extremely slow, but it never stopped the kids from lining up outside her door waiting to buy candy. So, I convinced Mrs. Hudson to give me a job assisting her for $3 per week. Not only was I a big help to Mrs. Hudson, I had the opportunity to find out why, after being robbed, she did not close her candy operation. She was making over $250 a week selling candy in a housing project. Back then, that was a lot of money.

However, I had bigger plans. I worked for Mrs. Hudson for about a month, and it didn't take me long to realize I was getting paid slave labor wages. So, I convinced my mom to invest some of our welfare money into starting a candy store in our apartment. It was not a hard sell, my mom invested, and I ran it. It was indeed a success. I know what you're thinking. "He put that old lady out of business and that's not right!" But keep in mind, it was a free enterprise and she was only paying me $3 a week.

Remember, true entrepreneurs can't be afraid of competition.

Our first week open, we made over $350. My mom was truly loving me. Don't tell any of my brothers and sisters, but I think I was her favorite child that week. But to make that business venture a success, I had to learn from someone with experience. I was 13 years old and never ran a candy store. However, I was willing to do whatever it took to learn - even if I had to work for only $3 per week. By the way, to make a long story short, we ran our candy store for four months strong until someone told the housing authority that we were running an illegal business operation from our low-income apartment. So, they made us close down the candy store, or move.

We closed down, but it was fun while it lasted.

Never be afraid, or too proud, to be mentored –True entrepreneurs have to be open to learning new ideas. From individuals who have already travel down the road of success.

I'm not saying go out and work with Your best friend to steal all of his business secrets to open your own business. However, if you're Interested in starting a business, Learn as much as you can from Someone that has experience, even If you have to work for pennies to get the experience. Trust me; it's worth it in the end.

I just conveyed a brief story as to How to be a good follower pays off. Now, let's focus on a good leader. My definition of a good leader is "a person that could motivate, encourage, or convince someone to perform a task even at times they don't want to do it".

Growing up in a Chicago housing project is growing up in a city within a city. We always did things to have fun even developing our own dance groups. Let's flash back to the days of break dancing.

Who could forget Pop-locking, the Break dancing or the spinning on your head?

Those were the days. That was a great business venture just waiting to happen. I remember how I started my first dance group. Of course, I was the captain. My dance name was Energizer Eveready Dra; however I could not break dance a lick! But, I knew how to lead my Peers. I recruited all the best break dancers in the neighborhood for my crew. I offered them that twist I spoke about in chapter one. I required all my dancers to pay dues of 25 cents a week. I bought us t-shirts and drew graffiti on them as we all had matching uniforms. In addition, on a weekly basis, we had house parties at each other's homes and charged 50 cents per person to all comers. We made between $50 to $75 per week with little overhead I was the leader, it was my idea, and I controlled the funds! My friends

were privileged to be in my group.
Many other kids from the
neighborhood tried to duplicate our
efforts, but they were not as
successful for many reasons,
one reason was lack of discipline.
As a kid, I already learned that in
order to be the best, I had to work
harder than my competition to be
successful. While the members of
other groups were out playing, my
group was practicing.

Therefore, when it came time for
competitions, we were the best! Our
work ethics showed a unified and
organized group. By winning these
competitions, it gave my peers the
faith and belief in my ability to lead.
Now let's remember, I was the
weakest and worst break dancer in
the group, however, I was the

strongest leader, hardest worker, and the number one motivator. Think about it! I got 13 year old kids to practice six days a week without adult supervision.

Remember, a true entrepreneur must be a great leader, a hard worker, and a strong motivator. Entrepreneur leads by example and the organization is only as strong as the individual that's running it.

Chapter Three:

Another Man's Junk Is an Entrepreneur's Treasurer

As you can see, I had a somewhat profitable and interesting childhood, nevertheless, every child must grow up, and I did it early. I had my first child at the age of 16 and my second at the age of 17. As a junior in high school, I had a family with all of the responsibilities.

What a culture shock! What did I do? You guessed it. I stepped up to the plate and took care of my responsibilities. Just imagine the pressure I was under and the pressure I put on myself. I was too proud to live at home. I felt I was in love, so I moved out of my mother's home, got my own apartment at the age of 17 with my girlfriend and our two children. I had to pay $155 a month for rent plus utilities, while still attending high school. I knew, if I didn't do anything else, I must get that high school diploma. Therefore, I put any visions of being an entrepreneur aside and secured my first and last W2 job.

I began working for our local park district making $5.50 per hour.

Doesn't sound like much – back then, minimum wage was $3.35 per hour. According to most, I was not doing badly for my first job at the age of 18. And you know what? I kind of liked that job too. It was easy work, and it had a few benefits as well. I worked there for a year – and never missed a day of work. However, something happened on that December 19th that changed my life forever. The boss called me into his office – I thought to receive our small Christmas bonus that everyone was talking about. I got a bonus alright, I got fired! With absolutely no true explanation whatsoever! Needless to say, I was hurt, distraught, disappointed, and I felt betrayed as well as angry.

And because of my pride, I could not go home and tell my girlfriend that I got fired. Therefore, for two weeks, I left each day as if going to work. Instead, I was hanging out in the streets with some bad elements and doing some bad things. I was hustling in the streets. Yes me! I knew it was wrong, but I had a family to take care of and I refused to see my kids go hungry. And sad to say I was good at it! However, God had another plan for me.

One day I was hanging with some friends, and they were talking about some guys making beds in an alley in Chicago and selling them to furniture stores, and making money doing it. You know me by now! They said making money. So I had to see this for myself. Check this out, and get this. These guys were collecting old mattresses and box springs, stripping the mattresses down to the springs, putting on new padding and covers and selling to stores at a wholesale price. They were making a huge profit. I was truly amazed! My entrepreneur drive and spirit was sparked again. For that reason, I studied those guys for a month. Then, I approached them about their venture. It was costing them $14 in materials to recondition the mattresses and box springs and they were selling them for $25 per set. The stores were retailing them on an average of $95 per set. I knew those guys were being taken advantaged of, so I offered them a solution they couldn't refuse. I bought their business idea for $1000. That was the best $1000 I ever spent...

Remember, to be an entrepreneur, you must have vision and you must be able to recognize and see a business opportunity through someone else's dream.

Keep in mind; I never made a mattress in my life. However, I had a willing group of guys working out of an alley with a proven trade that included collecting old mattresses that people trashed and recycling them for wholesale sales.

My friends laughed at those guys – my friends saw junk. But my entrepreneur eyes saw a hidden treasure. Guess what? I became that junk man I talked about earlier – I was driving up and down the streets and alleys in my pick up truck looking for old mattresses to recycle. And yes, you guessed it! My friends were laughing at me as well. I didn't care. I had my mind made up that no other individual would ever control my destiny. The only one that could stop you from being a successful entrepreneur is God and yourself. Yes, I'm guilty! I was indeed, looking for other people's junk to make it into my treasure.

Chapter 4

Count Up the Cost Before You Take the Loss *(keep your eye on the prize)*

Wow! My first real adult business venture and it was a perfect fit. I had a product, (recycled mattresses) a clientele, (furniture stores), ready-made employees, and a company name and slogan, **Best Rest Mattress** "Where You Get the Best Rest for Your Dollar". I was ready to tackle the bedding market with a vengeance.

As you can see, I have a knack for putting businesses together. However, it takes more than just putting businesses together that makes an entrepreneur successful. I was gun-ho about my business venture as well. I will never forget my first business card, "Leonard Hayes, Owner." It sounded good and it felt good; although, through my excitement, I forgot one very important thing, the most important thing of all, **counting up the cost**. I wasn't 13 years old anymore, selling candy and ice cups from home. This was the real world, with real bills, and dealing with real business people.

Never the less I found the perfect commercial building to rent in order to start my mattress empire. It was a huge warehouse space facility with an overhead bay door and equipped with a space for manufacturing the product as well. In addition, there was office space. I was well on my way. However, I did not factor in the first and last months' rent, security deposit, remodeling cost, signs, accountant fees to set up a corporation, office furniture, equipment and vehicles to deliver the product, and more. Prior to recycling one mattress, I was over $10,000 in the red and that was before materials were purchased to make the product. As you can imagine, that was a huge wake-up call.

Remember this A successful entrepreneur must a have a business plan. Count up the cost.

75% of small businesses fell because of lack of planning. If you don't do anything else research your business venture expenses first and leave run for unexpected expenses.

Yes, I had a product and clientele, but without money to cover the overhead, the idea was absolutely worthless. Statistics say two out of every three new businesses fail in the first year for this very reason – lack of planning and budgeting. Therefore, my survival skills took over, and I sold my idea and concept to a friend. He helped with the capital to finance the project and I was finally on my way.

Remember a true entrepreneur never quits! They always find a way to get the job done.

When we first started production, I had four employees, my partner, and myself. I was destined to make this project a success. It took us one month to make 50 sets of mattresses which I believed we were doing well. I remember driving to Chicago in a u-haul with a truck full of mattresses and my "Best Rest" emblem on the product – just trying to make my first sell to a store – the effort was a success! I sold every mattress on the truck to the first store I visited.

In addition, the store ordered an additional 50 sets which they wanted delivered within two weeks. I left with a $3000 check and a commitment for 50 additional sets. Wow! I was on top of the world until I got back and balanced my books. I realized my employees' salaries were $1300 and materials another $1400. I put in 60 hours a week for a month and only made a $300 profit – and had to split that with my partner. In addition, I still had the basic overhead of $2500 a month in bills. I soon realized why those guys were manufacturing from an alley. Yes, it was gut check indeed.

To be a successful entrepreneur, you have to be willing to take a knock out punch and be able to get up to fight again.

I was just hit with a body shot, but I got up swinging. I immediately realized where I went wrong. Although I had a great concept, my production was too slow. Therefore, I found better equipment to produce the product faster. I went from 50 sets a month to 50 sets every other week, with the same number of employees and overhead. The profit was a little better and the punches didn't hurt as badly.

Remember, to be a successful entrepreneur, you must be willing to count up the cost before you take a loss. And remember one important thing don't spend what you don't have.

I want you to remember this personal quote of which I made up myself "you can't see a vision with your eyes closed". It's so very true! By now, I'm two years in the mattress business, and I'm still not making a major profit, however, the word "quit" was not in my vocabulary. I still felt I had a great product with two years experience. I learned how to manufacture the product and had three major furniture stores buying my product.

Unfortunately, the relationship with my business partner did not last. He took his eyes off the prize, nevertheless, that worked out in my favor.

Later, I soon realized that those furniture stores were making the most profit, so I decided to go retail. I started **The Price Is Right Bedding Store** - it was an instant success. My eyes were closed for two years. I let all that retail money slip through my fingers. I went from $1500 a month to $1500 a week profit with the same product. Now that's an eye opener!

Remember to be a successful entrepreneur, you must be willing to keep your eyes on the prize and not give up. Diversify

yourself and learn how to maximize your product to the fullest.

I went from not only selling mattresses, but also bedding accessories as well. The retail business was going so well that I wanted to expand it. Thus, I opened another bedding store on a college campus that was a success as well. However, with every success story there is some heartache. Keeping your eye on the prize can be difficult when you have employees stealing you blind. Here is a news flash. Don't mix money with sticky fingers- I found that out the hard way. For every three sets of mattresses I was selling through the front door, my employees were selling two sets out the back door. And, they were not selling it for the business. Yeah you guess it they was robbing me blind; Needless to say, I fired the thieves. To this day, I still wonder just how much they stole from my company. I continued the retail stores for another year, after that, it was time for me to move on to my next venture.

Remember, to be successful in your business, you need to know the people you hire. And let them earn your trust. Don't give it away so easily, And always keep a close watch on your inventory.

Remember keep your eye on the prize and on your money as well.

Chapter 5

Business and Family Do Not Mix

Growing up with nine brothers and sisters in a household was very exciting; we had our own baseball team. I enjoyed the family barbeques and I never had to worry about losing a fight because we always had backup. On the other hand, I wish family felt the same way about business, which brings me to another business venture.

Remember, a true entrepreneur always seeks out business opportunities wherever they go and never run away from a challenge – an entrepreneur runs to it.

One summer day, I stopped by a store and noticed a "For Rent" sign in a restaurant window. I peeked inside the window and noticed a fully-equipped restaurant with all the bells and whistles. I instantly knew this was a gold mine. However, I did learn something as indicated in chapter four; I counted up the cost before I took a loss. I called the phone number to inquire about the restaurant. To my amazement, the restaurant was in excellent shape and the owner only wanted $450 per month rent that included all the fixtures as well. I just could not pass up this great business opportunity as the restaurant was located across the street from a night club. Therefore, I came up with a concept and a great name **The Snack Shack,** "You Snack It, We Pack It". And largely due to the fact, there was bullet-proof glass; I wanted to keep the restaurant open 24 hours. In addition, there was no nearby competition.

I had great location, wonderful concept, and excellent opportunity. All I had to do now was hire the staff. What greater staffing possibilities are there when you have nine loving brothers and sisters, we could cover all three shifts. And, if you have to pay someone to work for you anyway, why not pay family. One of my sisters had restaurant experience and her husband loved to cook, and my other brothers and sisters could cook as well. We conducted our family meeting and we were well on our way to a successful restaurant business.

To stock the restaurant cost me $1000, which was great. I just knew I struck another gold mine (if you spend $1000 on food in the restaurant business your return is $3500). This was a pretty nice profit. We had the best polish sausages in town and our chicken wings were a best seller. Our first day open we made $250 the first shift, $300 the second shift, and $550 the third shift. I made my investment back the first week in business – this was great! And, on the weekends, we made over $3000. I knew I stumbled on the goose that laid the golden egg. I was so excited! The first few months of the business was going great. Then again, I soon realized that business and family don't mix.

The one thing that I learned about the restaurant business is that it is, indeed, a cash cow. You would have thought I had learned my lesson from my last business venture in regards to trust and watching my money. But even the best entrepreneur can be naïve when it comes to family, and I was just that! All of a sudden, I noticed I was buying more food and making less profit. You guessed it. My family was stealing, or at least that's what I thought. Consequently, this put me in a tough spot. First, I didn't want to believe that my own family would steal from me after I provided such a great opportunity for us all; and second, I didn't know who was stealing. It was family, I didn't want to accuse the wrong person and cause animosity or hurt feelings among my siblings. Nevertheless, I knew something had to be done! Or, I would have had to stop snacking and start packing.

Remember, to be a true entrepreneur you must be willing to make tough decisions and you must be willing to accept the consequences that come as a result of the decisions you make.

The first thing I did was to examine myself. What did I do wrong? It was obvious. I was not there to run my business. I worked at the restaurant probably two hours day, and that was a huge mistake. Yes my sister, had restaurant experience but she never ran a business. A true entrepreneur must show his or her leadership skills at all times. Remember, this is your vision, not the vision of your employees. As a result, I started being there more often, and it did not take long for me to start finding problems. My first problem was my family was eating up the profits. Food was our product, and every time they got hungry they ate - so just imagine six people eating 2 to 3 meals a day, that's 18 meals a day, and 90 orders a week taken out of the business. As you can imagine, that put a sizeable dent in our profit. Subsequently, I did something that I should have been done from day one - provide structure.

Due to the fact, they were not putting money into the business, the bottom line was not as important to them as it was to me. Needless to say, some of my siblings had a problem with me immediately in this regard. They felt I was trying to run things. News flash! I was the one spending the money on the business, it was my idea, I was the entrepreneur, and I was obligated to run it! That's when I realized they only respected me as their little brother and not as a businessman. For years, my siblings held animosity toward me because of the decisions I made regarding that particular business venture.

Do, I regret hiring my family? Yes! And No! Yes, because my family's love for me is more important than money. And no, because they needed to know that their little brother was, indeed, a businessman in every sense that defines an entrepreneur and they must learn to respect that. I am not saying that you should never hire family members. As a matter of fact, some of my siblings still work for me this very day. But because of the stand I took then, I now have their respect as a boss, I've earned their respect as an entrepreneur, and I still have their love as a little brother.

Remember, a true entrepreneur must earn respect and be respectful .... A company is only as strong as the person running it. You can't be afraid of making decisions based on feelings. Feelings don't pay the bills profits do.

Chapter 6

Leave the Leeches Behind

My high school senior year book indicates that I was voted the "least likely to succeed." Well, I guess I let a lot of folks down that I knew during my high school years. I'm doing pretty well for myself these days. Not bragging; Just fact. Unfortunately, you realize that in many instances, along with success comes leeches. My definition of leech is: "<u>blood sucking worms that</u>

<u>sucks the blood out of you and will
not let go until all the blood is gone."</u>

***To be a successful entrepreneur
you must associate with people
that have similar mind set, goals
and visions.***

By now, I realized that I had a knack for business and my peers were convinced of the same. All of sudden, I was Mr. Popular, Leonard Hayes, the entrepreneur. I must admit, it felt good to receive all that attention, and I had all those cool friends that I wished I had in high school. Unfortunately, I soon realized my cool friends did not care about me as a person at all; they only cared about how much money I could make them. In knowing that, it brings me to another business venture.

I purchased my very first home from my uncle by use of a land contract. That house needed a lot of work. In fact, it was an absolute dump! However, I'm always up for a challenge, and unbeknown to my uncle, he just introduced me to something that would, indeed, change by entire life forever – the real estate business.

One day at home, I received a call from a telemarketer about securing a mortgage in order to refinance my house. I told the lady, "I didn't have a current mortgage to refinance, although, I had this thing called a "land contract." She told me she could utilize the land contract, pay off my uncle, and provide me with $15,000 "cash out" for my pocket. In addition, my monthly payments would be lower than what I was currently paying my uncle. My next question was "how much will this cost me"? She replied, "Nothing"! I told her to do it! To my amazement, I received a check for $13,500 within 30 days, and from that moment, I knew I was on to something good.

I asked the mortgage representative "how was this possible?" The reply was "equity." The company used the equity available in the property to provide me with a pay-off to my uncle as well as cash money in my pocket.

Although, I was a pretty smart businessman, that "equity" thing went right over my head. Nevertheless, I enjoyed the $13,000 in my pocket, I asked her if I could repeat what had been done, she said yes so I immediately purchased another house. My second real-estate transaction secured me with a check for $20,000 – I was on a roll.

However again, I made another crucial mistake – I could not keep my mouth shut. I was so excited about the concept, I told all my, you know, so-called friends about this new business venture, and it spread like wild fire. I had every Mike, James, and John questioning me about real estate, and guess what?

I told them the secret. The next thing I knew, my friends were attempting to saturate the market I identified for myself and steel my vision. It got so serious; they were fist fighting over property.

One day I met a lady who had 21 properties near foreclosure and that was the day I hit the real-estate jackpot. The lady's husband left her these properties at foreclosure status – he also ran off with a younger woman. (But that's another story) He financed this deed by mortgaging the properties for $100,000 in cash and ran off with the money. Fortunately for me, I saw a real opportunity to capitalize on a bad situation. I offered the lady $120,000 for all the properties and she accepted. Little did she know that each property was worth approximately $60,000. Wow! Was right! I just purchased $1.2 million dollars worth of property for $120,000 – that was better than hitting the lottery – at least that's what I thought.

I learned the hard way – to be a successful entrepreneur, you cannot save the world. And you must learn how to analyze the people's motive that you associate yourself with.

I proceeded to secure mortgages on three of the properties as the remaining 18 houses were paid for free and clear.

Unfortunately, those leeches got the best of me once again. I reached out to every one of my so-called friends to inform them I was selling my houses wholesale. They each walked away from the closing table with approximately $30,000 cash without spending a dime. Yes, I made OK money; however, my friends literally killed the market. They did not understand that this money was not free – it was a loan. They got the money and never repaid the loans – most all of those houses went into foreclosure once again. What comes next, you will never believe. All those leeches had the nerve to say it was my fault because I took advantage of them – they knew nothing about real estate. However, they knew how to spend that money. This was a clear example of a "fool and his money will soon depart."

Just think! If I would have kept my mouth shut and stopped trying to win a popularity contest, how much money I would have made. Every one of those guys lost their homes. One year later, they were back where I found them – broke and working a nine to five. I learned a valuable lesson – you don't ever have to forget where you came from, but you can surely forget the folks that mean you no good. All those leeches were out for one thing, and that was to suck the blood out of me. What the devil meant for bad, God made it work out for my good. I even repurchased some of those same houses that I sold those guys and made a profit all over again. I went on to buy and rehabilitate well over 80 houses, making hundreds and thousands of dollars; and I did it without leeches. Remember, "A mistake only hurts if you continue to make it." I made my mistake by carrying leeches and I'm proud to say today I am leech free.

Remember, to be a successful entrepreneur you must leave those leeches behind. And you must be willing to learn from your mistakes.

Chapter 7

Know When To Fold 'Em

Let's take a walk down memory lane. Do you remember that first VCR that cost $799 or how about that first five-pound brick cellular phone. Wow how technology has changed. Today, you can purchase a VCR for 29 bucks and obtain a cell phone the size of a credit card. When I acquired my first cell phone, I had to put down a $500 deposit and the minutes were 50 cents each. I recall saying "man they are ripping me off; I need to get into that business." This brings us to another business venture.

Back in the early 90s, technology was on the rise, computers were beginning to be even more popular, and we could not live without pagers – everyone had one. It only cost $10 per month with voice mail and it was the "in thing" to have. Being popular had its advantages; you could sometimes get special treatment. On one occasion upon paying my pager bill, the owner of the store asked me to come to his back office to speak with him. Unbeknown to him at the time, I was very impressed; this brother had a first-class pager operation. He had state-of-the-art equipment and repair center, and he had the only pager store in the whole city. There was mutual respect between us - I found that he was impressed with me as well – because of my real estate dealings. I had something he wanted and he had something I wanted, therefore, we swapped ideas.

To my surprise, he had another hidden treasurer. He was charging $20 for activation, $10 a month for air time, and $5 for late fees. In addition, he was acquiring the pagers themselves for $1 each. This guy was making money hand over fist. And, let's not forget those costly repairs for which he was charging as well. I believe this was the first young entrepreneur that I ran across whom I admired both his business skill and vision. I took his idea and was soon on my way to starting my own pager company, but it was not cheap. By the way, this guy charged by $2500 to teach me the basics, and I paid it. I just knew with the right location, I could make a huge profit.

Remember, to be a successful entrepreneur you have to realize that knowledge is power and sometimes knowledge does not come cheap.

This guy was, indeed, very smart! He made me sign a none-competition clause so I would not take over this territory. I did that as well. I should have brought this guy on as a partner, he was pretty sharp. I had the product, now I needed a clientele. What better place than a college campus. COMMUNICATION TECHNOLOGY IS HUGE WITH COLLEGE STUDENTS. College students don't usually have much money, and at that time, cell phones were not affordable, however pagers were ideal. There were no other pager stores on campus, consequently I had no competition. In addition, the twist included combining the store with hip hop clothing.

It was a great idea, in a great location; unfortunately, this idea had a few holes in it. College students were only in school eight months out of a year - which would leave four months down time. And, the real estate was expensive around campus contributing to high overhead as well as a long driving distance from my home. None of this stopped me. I secured a partner to help carry the financial load. A partner is a good option if you choose the right one. My partner and I proceeded to set up the operation for a cellular/pager and clothing operation – great marketing plan and great operation. We secured 50 pager customers within the first 30 days, unfortunately, we ran into a few minor problems and one major problem. Our high-end, hip-hop clothing lines did not sell as well as we had hoped. We did not do our research in this regard. College students do not care about name brand clothes - they only care about eating, sleeping, studying, and partying. We had a big problem, indeed. There was over $25,000 in clothing inventory that we could not sell, and I had a business partner more concerned about the college girls and the fame of being a business owner than the business itself. He was always late and he eventually ran out of money, leaving me with the entire financial burden.

Remember, a smart entrepreneur does his research first and makes his purchase later. And when picking a partner in

business, make sure you share the same values, business sense and financial means to help your venture grow.

You would have thought by now, I would know better – as we continue to live, we continue to learn. For the next nine months, my sweet smelling cash cow was turning into a skunk smelling money pit. So what did I do? I downsized.

Remember, a true entrepreneur knows when to cut their losses. Never be afraid to downsize. You would rather run a smaller business then no business at all.

I kept the pager and cellular portion of the store, liquidated all of the clothing, moved to a smaller location around the corner from the campus, and got rid of my partner. I just wish I would have done this a year earlier. By now the damage was done. I sank over $100,000 of my own money in the project, and because it was such a long distance from my home, the business began to create a strain on my family life. Plus, a competitor came into my territory, undercut my prices, and stole half my customers. Again, what did I do? You guessed it. I folded up camp and went back to what I do best, real estate. Was I disappointed because I closed down this particular business? No, it was a learning experience and a trade.

Remember, to be a successful entrepreneur, you must be willing to be a risk taker. And you can't be afraid of failure. You never know the outcome of a venture if you don't take the risk. And remember this too! A lot of people will not even start the race, let alone finish it. If your business venture fails, its OK – at least you finished the race. However, be smart and know when to fold 'em. And one thing about folding is that you can always be dealt another hand.

Chapter 8

When Your Back Is Up Against the Wall

If there is any chapter in this book that was hard to right, it was this one. You can clearly see, as I put my life's story on paper, my past business venture's includes a tremendous amount of battle scars. However, the scars I obtained from what follows nearly destroyed me. For the very first time in my life, I was faced with an obstacle that my entrepreneur and business skills could not help me with - that was my marriage. Being an entrepreneur, in this respect, put a tremendous strain on my marriage. My wife wanted out! Not because I was unfaithful instead, I was never home. I soon realized I was married to my business and not to my wife. In addition, I also realized that when a woman falls out of love it's over; you can't buy it back, and you can't negotiate it back. I was up against something with which my business finesse could not help, that was facing a divorce.

For the very first time in my life, I felt helpless; my family was my life. This was the woman I had been with since high school and the mother of my three children. We had been together for 13 years. We were both active in our church, and I really thought the rough times were behind us. Now don't get me wrong, I'm not saying I was an angel throughout our 13-year relationship; I did make some vital mistakes. There were indeed, times when she should have left. However, when I got right with God, I tried to be the best God-fearing husband I could possibly be. I soon learned that it is hard to focus on business when your heart is broken. Consequently, my life began to move in a downward spiral.

The pager store put a strain on me financially as well, and I couldn't focus on making money. I was broke with no hope. And, my so-called friends, colleagues, leeches, or whatever you want to call them, were all gone by now. I had no one to call on but God. Through it all, I never blamed God; instead, God gave me a new revelation about life.

God revealed to me that all I needed to do was trust Him and serve Him. If it's God's will, then its God's bill; He will provide. I must admit, it was a humbling experience. I came to understand that God was not getting the true glory for all He was doing, and had done, in my life. People were giving glory to me, so maybe that is why God stripped me down. I know, this may sound strange, but I'm glad He did.

That was a rough year for me. I had to face many demons from my past as well. One of those demons was my father. My father was never there for me. He was an alcoholic and abusive and maybe that is why I wanted to be accepted by everyone with whom I came in contact. It was tough being rejected by someone who was supposed to love and protect you. I had built up a strong hatred in my heart for that man, still God had a plan. While I was going through my divorce, I received a call from a relative that my father was homeless and living on the streets of Chicago. My first thought was "why was this relative calling me?" However, God quickly directed my spirit to go find him. I was obedient to God's will, and I went.

As I drove up and saw him, tears began to stream down my face. My father was, indeed, living in a doorway of an abandoned building. He had one bag that contained all his worldly possessions. My heart went from hatred to love, instantly. I immediately embraced him with a hug and told him I loved him. You guessed it? I took him home with me and gave him a place to live. God's timing is not our timing and for this reason, unbeknown to either of us, my father was terminally ill with cancer. He died within six months after I brought him home. I took care of all the funeral arrangements and the associated costs; there was no life insurance policy. As I laid my father to rest, I saw what God had done. He provided me with an opportunity to face one of my most horrible demons that allowed for so many other demons to become a large part of my life. They were hiding inside me. God began to heal those old wounds and released those demons.

After I buried my father, I finally concluded that my marriage was officially over, and my wife and I proceeded to file for a divorce. Although I was broke, I was still a businessman, so we compromised. She wanted a man that was there all the time and I wanted my children to grow up in a stable financial environment. It's very hard to understand women, they say they want financial security, but some women don't want to sacrifice to get it. There are two types of men in this world: a man that makes a lot of money generally does not have a lot of time; and a man that has a lot of time, generally, does not make a lot of money. Needless to say, my wife left me for a broke dude. But, don't despair! She did me a huge favor, she willingly gave me custody of my children and the Lord was on His way to help me rebuild my life. I'm sad to say, I don't have any entrepreneur points to give you in this chapter. Nevertheless, I do have some spiritual advice. As you go through the hustles of this hexed road of striving to become an entrepreneur, don't forget to stop and pray, listen to God. Maybe, just maybe, He's trying to tell you something.

__Remember this while you are struggling to be an entrepreneur you must maintain a balance between business and family. Your family needs you to survive just like that business does.__

Chapter 9

Taking No Prisoners

I'm broke, a single parent with three kids, and 20 pounds lighter due to stress. However, I have two important possessions in my custody, God and an entrepreneur spirit. It was time to get busy and I was **taking no prisoners.** I had already identified my niche, it was real estate, but in order to purchase real estate you need money and good credit. Naturally, I had neither at this time due to the divorce. A true entrepreneur knows how to improvise. So I did. I had come to the realization about those mortgage brokers who were providing me with loans; they were making a nice profit off of me, not to mention the referral business that I provided as well. My loan officer's salary was approximately $250,000 per year, just securing loans. I knew I was smarter and brighter than he was; which brings me to another business venture.

Remember, a true entrepreneur must know how to improvise and be willing to step out on faith. Never be afraid to change your career.

I decided that I was going to reinvent my self as a mortgage broker. I dressed up in my best suit and proceeded to hunt for a job in this field. One thing about becoming a mortgage broker, any company will hire you; its 100% commission salary, the company can't lose. It's up to you to bring in the clientele. If you don't work, you don't eat. I was hired by the first company I sought after. I really impressed that lady. I was well dressed, professional, and my real estate background provided me with enough knowledge about mortgages to speak the lingo. I took advantaged of the opportunity and negotiated a commission of 65%, a huge split for a rookie loan officer.

Although, I was an excellent negotiator, I realized that being a mortgage broker was much more than taking applications and collecting documents. It took me three months before I closed my first deal. We almost starved, and my Neon was repossessed as well. I knew I could be successful in this business, and within six months I was the top producer in the company.

Again, my entrepreneur juices began to flow. I was receiving a nice commission split, and I was in demand as well. My production skills were top notch, and I began to market myself to the highest bidder, whoever was going to pay me the most money was where my loyalty lays .So I began employment with the competitor across the street. This company paid me 75%. This was absolutely fantastic! My only problem, after a year in this business, revealed I knew more than the owner. It is extremely difficult for a natural born leader to follow a weak boss. I had to do something quickly. Keep in mind, I was, and still am, a God-fearing young man who had a tremendous amount of experience running my own businesses. In this instance, I respect another man's decisions about his vision, therefore, I ventured out on my own.

I negotiated with a company to pay me 85% commission and the organization was willing to allow me to work off of its license as well as work from home. In my opinion, this was a great start. I was technically my own boss, and I was able to be home for the kids when they got out of school. This was perfect! I had no furniture in my living room, this worked out well. I acquired a desk, two chairs, a fax machine, and found an old copy machine. I created my first mortgage company out of my living room. Was that creative or what? I closed four deals a month and was making at least $7000 per month working from home. Then, I knew I was in the right field of work.

One day, a couple of colleagues came over to visit with me. They were unhappy with the company for which they currently worked. My colleagues knew I had the know-how and the skills to be extremely successful in this business. As a result, they wanted to work with me, out of my home as well. There was another business just waiting to happen, another vision. Once I brought these guys into my operation, provided them with a place to work, and trained them correctly, it would mean additional income for myself. Accordingly, I found office space that I shared with another company, a 12 ft x 12 ft room, and I shared the room with four employees – this was the start of my mortgage empire.

Before I hired those guys, I gave them some serious advice as to my way of thinking, it is as follows: "trust and loyalty are very important to me, and as long as you don't allow greed to creep into your eye sight, you will be successful." I'm happy to say that those guys took that advice and we have not looked back since.

They worked hard and followed my instructions to a "T". We started to grow faster than I anticipated as other brokers wanted to join our team. I did what any smart businessman would do; I expanded and secured a larger location. When I found the perfect location, I took my loan officers to see it. They were in absolute awe! They said, "What are we going to do with all this space?" We expanded from 144 sq.

ft. to 1500 sq. ft. I said, "We will fill it up with loan officers."

Remember, a true entrepreneur sees the vision first and must have the drive to bring the vision to fruition.

Now I had a great location, and I had a crew. However, I also had one major concern, larger overhead. My company was receiving 85% of the commission from the current organization we represented and I needed more. For this reason, I negotiated with another company and secured 100% of the commission minus an administrative fee. I was taking no prisoners. That first year, in this location, I made over $800,000 in fees and my staff grew to over 15 loan officers after a year and a half. Once again, I had to expand. Good people will follow you if you know how to lead and I was a good, strong leader. I developed structured rules, conducted weekly meetings, and I had a compassionate heart. Nevertheless, I was stern when it came to business. I even had a weekly dress code. I felt that if you dress for success, you will work for success. I live by this rule to this very day. By the third year at that location, I was at 25 loan officers strong and making over $2 million in fees a year. That's taking no prisoners.

Remember, to be a true entrepreneur, you must be willing to fight for what you believe in and know that you can over come any obstacle that comes your way. Oh yes, take no prisoners.

Wow! I came back with a vengeance. I'm running a successful mortgage company, I built a beautiful home for my family, I got remarried, and I'm making more money than I've ever made in my entire life. I am indeed, a visionary. Let's define visionary; "<u>someone who has foresight, in other words, someone who sees things before it happens.</u>" That's me! It's the gift God gave me, and I am extremely grateful to have it.

At this point, I'm now three years into the mortgage business, and things are great! I'm maxed out on office space, and for once in my life, I was starting to feel complete. However, I had one issue, I was not content.

Remember, a true entrepreneur is never content with their status quo, always strive for more.

Unfortunately, I was leasing from a slum lord. The air conditioner did not work in the summer and the heat did not work in the winter. And, I was beginning to hear the grumbles and complaints from the employees. Naturally, they were looking to me to fix the problem. What was I going to do? I had to do something quickly, of course. My staff was making all the money. It's easy to understand that a happy office is a productive office. And, for this reason, I went out to make the folks as happy as possible.

My bigger vision included acquiring a more comfortable environment for my employees. This time, I did not want to lease; I wanted to own the facility. No more throwing money down the drain. I was in the mortgage business, did I not believe in my own product? Of course I believed in my product, I believed in myself, and most important I believed in my vision. For these reasons, I went searching for the ultimate new location and I found it!

I found an 18,000 sq. ft. office facility in a great location; easy to get to, great curb appeal, and only 15 minutes from my home. It was another gift from God. However, the asking price was $1.2 million. I had never made a purchase of that magnitude before in my life. I must admit, for the first time being an entrepreneur, business fear and doubt gripped my heart. I got the "what ifs" you know, what if I can't afford it, what if the loan officers don't get the loan approved, and so on and so forth. Yet, God quickened my spirit and reminded me if its Gods will, then its God's bill; that was all the comfort I needed. I quickly went home and told my wife about the building. She was excited as well, until I provided her with the negative points about the project. Commercial requires 30% down payment which is $345,000 cash plus $20,000 in closing costs and not to mention $50,000 build-out costs, $75,000 for furniture, and $15,000 mortgage payment per month. This is close to another one-half million dollars, which would have wiped us out financially; our whole life's savings at the time.

But my wife understood my vision, so she put the ball in my court, and you know what? I took the shot! I offered a contract for $1.1 million and it was accepted. It took two months before the place opened for business, but I finally did it. God had to truly prepare me for what I had to face next; I realized that not everyone likes change. In fact, some people actually fear change when you take them out of a comfort zone. This, in turn, provided problems and issues in the office regarding some of my employees. Sadly, these problems came from some of my seasoned employees which were very surprising. They knew where I brought us from, that I never lead us down a deserted road in the past, therefore, why would I do it now? God revealed that this vision was given to me, not to them. How could I expect all my staff to understand my vision, if they couldn't see it? God instructed me to just continue to lead, and He would guide me. That is exactly what I did.

Unfortunately, I did lose some key individuals, not because I did anything wrong, because fear gripped their hearts. I admit, this was a difficult transition, but God saw me through once again. My company grew from 25 employees to 45 employees, and I have one of the biggest mortgage companies in the south suburbs of Chicago. Now it was time to begin developing other business ventures as a result of this success, and I did!

Remember, a true entrepreneur must run with the vision without wavering, murmuring, or complaining. And remember this you're the boss. Never let your employees dictate to you how to run your business.

Chapter 10

A New Vision

Following your gut in business is very important, however being sensitive to the Holy Spirit is more important. This brings me to the last chapter of this book. I knew God had brought birth to this business and I knew He was going to continue to provide for my needs. But one day, God really put me to the test. I got a call from a group of doctors. They were inquiring about possibly buying my building. I told them that anything was for sale, and I would entertain an offer. I set up an appointment to meet with them. One morning, a doctor and the group's representative came to my office to look around as they were very much interested in the facility. They made an offer of $1.6 million which was a half million more than what I paid, and I only had the building for six months with an outstanding balance of $780,000. The difference would be all mines. I truly thought this was another Gift from God.

However, before I made this decision, I evaluated the situation very carefully. I had 40 full time employees working for me, where would they go and what was I going to do after the mortgage company? I was really torn, so I did the smart thing, I prayed. And the Lord shared with me that NCS Mortgage was to be the blessing for others as well as myself. Any future blessings for me, personally, would come from somewhere else. God instructed me not to sell. Sometimes, it is not for us to understand exactly what God is saying, just be obedient to His word, which brings me to another business venture.

God knows I could have used that half million, however the next plan God put in place was absolutely brilliant. When God gives you something, He writes the vision and provides the plan. God gave me the business venture of the year called New Vision Construction. Just as I stated in the previous chapters of this book, my passion is real estate, and I know my fortune lies in real estate as well. The puzzling question was "how was I going to get there?" The answer was "new construction". Contractors were building homes all over the country and I needed to tap into this market. I did just that! I noticed that the huge trend in real estate dealt with middle and upper class homeowners. This is great! However, the forgotten market was the average blue-collar, working class individual. So, I came up with this idea. What if I could build a beautiful four bedroom home for the average family, provide the financing, and price the house so it was affordable. It was a brilliant plan.

Now, I am also in the construction business. It cost money to build homes. I needed a partner, so I found one. Ironically, it was my neighbor who was the first to believe in the vision that God gave me and we proceeded to build our first home together. This first effort was a real challenge. Neither of us had ever built a house before and didn't know what to expect, but through hard work we succeeded. I had a perfect idea, I had a great location, I had a market, and now I needed more capital. The Lord sent me a word partnership, and not only did He send me a word, He sent me the right person to partner with. This guy was sharp, he was a thinker, and he had charisma. Actually, he reminded me of myself. He was a humble entrepreneur that did not have an ego problem or a problem with being a part of someone else's vision. Finally, I was not on an island alone anymore, I was beginning to build a city. New Vision Construction was on its way.

We came up with a unique wealth-building concept that not only changed peoples' lives financially, but it changed communities as well. Instead of having one partner, we obtained 30 partners, and New Vision Construction was now a major player in the construction industry.

Our concept was simple, we demonstrated to people just how to see our vision, invest their money, and build wealth through new construction.

I finally realized that the entrepreneur gift that God provided was not just for me. It was a tool in order that I become a blessing for others as well. I must say, this program has the beginnings of great success. Our partners helped us raise over $1 million in 90 days. God can really move. New Vision is in place to build over 200 homes within two years. This will provide 200 renters with homeownership, many for the very first time.

Remember, a true entrepreneur must not only see the vision, but must also be willing to share the vision as well.

Wow! I cannot believe what I just did. I wrote a book in seven days, and if you're reading this part – that means you read it all. Now Did I write this book to be a best seller? No. Did I write this book to acquire a multi-million dollar book deal? No. Did I write this book to brag about my accomplishments? No. God knows I made some terrible mistakes in business. I wrote this book because God told me to tell my real life experiences to real people. My prayer is that at least one thing was said to encourage, uplift, and motivate you or someone else to follow their dreams, no matter where it takes you. If I don't sell one book, it's OK! I just want to encourage you and say yes,

ENTREPRENEURESHIP IS A STRUGGLE, HOWEVER YOU CAN MAKE IT!